WILD HORSES

by Katie Marsico

Children's Press®

An Imprint of Scholastic Inc.

New York Toronto London Auckland Sydney
Mexico City New Delhi Hong Kong
Danbury, Connecticut

Content Consultant
Dr. Stephen S. Ditchkoff
Professor of Wildlife Sciences
Auburn University
Auburn, Alabama

Photographs © 2013: age fotostock/Zoonar/Katho Menden:
4, 5 background, 20; Alamy Images: 32 (blickwinkel/Hecker),
27 (Helge Schulz/Premium Stock Photography GmbH), 35 (Joe
Austin Photography); Bob Italiano: 44 foreground, 45 foreground;
Dreamstime/Ivan Chuyev: 2 background, 3 background, 44
background, 45 background; Media Bakery/Jeff Vanuga: 19; Photo
Researchers/J.-L. Klein & M.-L. Hubert: 5 bottom, 12; Shutterstock, Inc.:
8 (Grobler du Preez), 36 (loflo69); Superstock, Inc.: cover, 28 (age
fotostock), 39 (Don Johnston/age fotostock), 11 (Jörgen Larsson/age
fotostock), 24 (Minden Pictures), 1, 2 foreground, 3 foreground, 7, 23,
31, 40, 46 (NaturePL), 5 top, 16 (NHPA), 15 (Wolfgang Kaehler).

Library of Congress Cataloging-in-Publication Data
Marsico, Katie, 1980–
    Wild horses / by Katie Marsico.
        pages cm.–(Nature's children)
    Audience: 9–12.
    Audience: Grade 4 to 6.
    Includes bibliographical references and index.
    ISBN 978-0-531-20983-7 (lib. bdg.)
    ISBN 978-0-531-24309-1 (pbk.)
    1. Wild horses—Juvenile literature. 2. Horses—Juvenile literature. I. Title.
    SF360.M37 2013
    636.1'3—dc23   2012034333

All rights reserved. Published in 2013 by Children's Press, an imprint
of Scholastic Inc.
Printed in the United States of America 141
SCHOLASTIC, CHILDREN'S PRESS, and associated logos are
trademarks and/or registered trademarks of Scholastic Inc.

1 2 3 4 5 6 7 8 9 10 R 22 21 20 19 18 17 16 15 14 13

Wild Horses

Class	Mammalia
Order	Perissodactyla
Family	Equidae
Genus	*Equus*
Species	*Equus ferus* (wild horses), *Equus caballus* (domesticated horses)
World distribution	Africa, Asia, Australia, Europe, North America, and South America
Habitat	Primarily open grasslands; also found in coastal areas, deserts, forests, mountains, and wetlands
Distinctive physical characteristics	Coat colored in various shades of black, brown, gray, and white; coat also features patterns, including spots and light stripes, and is generally not as well-groomed as that of domesticated breeds; narrow head with large eyes; smaller than most domesticated horses; tough, thick hooves
Habits	Bond by nuzzling each other; communicate by making noises that include whinnies, snorts, squeals, and even screams; live in herds broken into smaller bands; begin mating between the ages of four and five; travel up to 20 miles (32 kilometers) a day to locate land where they can graze; generally live between 10 and 15 years in the wild
Diet	Prefer to graze on grass, but will also eat berries, fruits, leaves, twigs, and tree bark

Contents

CHAPTER 1

Running Wild, Roaming Free

Dawn breaks, and another summer day begins in the Sand Wash Basin in northwestern Colorado. A few crickets continue to quietly chirp as the sun rises. Grass and short bushes blanket the ground as far as the eye can see. The stillness of this peaceful landscape is broken by the sounds of whinnying and of hooves pounding the dusty ground.

A **herd** of American mustangs has arrived to **graze** in the basin. As these majestic horses feed on prairie grasses, an occasional ripple of activity disrupts their early-morning meal. Two mustangs pause to **groom** one another. A few **foals** run a short distance before stopping to play. A little farther off, a pair of **stallions** rear up on their hind legs and snort into the cool, dry air. The American mustangs in Sand Wash Basin are one of several herds of free-roaming horses that live in the wild today.

Herds of wild horses roam the plains of several different countries.

Wild Horses' Habitats

People often use the word wild to describe feral animals. Feral horses are the free-roaming relatives of domesticated herds. Their ancestors were domesticated horses that somehow managed to escape captivity. Over time, they learned to survive in the wilderness.

Wild horses exist on every continent except for Antarctica. In general, they prefer to graze in open grasslands. But they have also adapted to a wide variety of other habitats. Herds of wild horses can be found in deserts, mountains, forests, wetlands, and coastal areas.

For example, Cumberland Island horses that live off the southern coast of Georgia spend much of their time walking along salty marshes and sandy stretches of shoreline. Meanwhile, wild horses in southwestern Africa roam the vast Namib Desert. The desert is so dry that these horses sometimes experience 72-hour stretches when they are not able to drink any water. Luckily, they are equipped with remarkable survival skills.

Water is a scarce resource for the wild horses of the Namib Desert.

How Many Hands?

Horse experts use a special unit of measurement to determine equine height. This unit is known as the hand. One hand equals roughly 4 inches (10 centimeters). A horse's height is a measurement of the distance from its withers to the ground. The withers are the highest part of the horse's back at the base of its neck.

Wild horses are not all the same size. One of the shortest wild horse breeds is the Gotland pony. This breed is found on a Swedish island in the Baltic Sea. The average height of a Gotland pony is about 12 hands, or 4 feet (1.2 meters). Other wild horses, including American mustangs and Australian brumbies, often measure up to 15 hands, or 5 feet (1.5 m). This is still much shorter than the tallest domesticated horse, which holds a record height of more than 20 hands, or 6.7 feet (2 m). Most wild horses weigh between 800 and 1,100 pounds (360 and 500 kilograms).

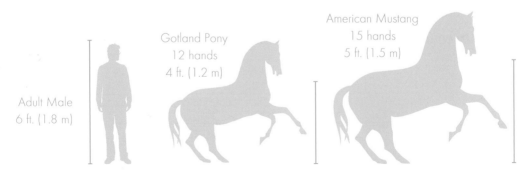

Adult Male
6 ft. (1.8 m)

Gotland Pony
12 hands
4 ft. (1.2 m)

American Mustang
15 hands
5 ft. (1.5 m)

The Gotland ponies of Sweden are smaller than most other wild horses.

Alike, Yet Different

Most wild horses look a lot like their domesticated relatives. Members of wild herds, though, are not always perfectly groomed. This is because they roam across rugged habitats and do not receive any human care.

Wild horses are various shades of white, brown, gray, and black. Some are marked with spots or faint stripes. All horses have long hair growing off of their neck. This is called a mane. They also have a patch of hair called a forelock between their ears. Most wild horses have long, narrow heads with large eyes and pointed ears. Like all ungulates, they have hoofed feet.

Smaller horses—both wild and domesticated—are often called ponies. They tend to have different physical features than those of larger horses. For example, ponies frequently have a thicker mane, tail, and coat. In addition, a pony's head, neck, and body are shorter and wider. Larger horses also tend to have longer, leaner legs.

Some wild horses are marked with interesting patterns.

CHAPTER 2

From Tamed to Untamed

All wild horses share one important quality. They have all adapted to life in the wilderness. Domesticated animals depend on people to feed them or provide land where they can graze. These horses generally spend time in stables, pens, or some type of closed pasture or range. This helps protect them from wild animals and extreme weather conditions. In many cases, veterinarians are available to treat any illnesses or health risks that domesticated horses face.

The ancestors of today's wild breeds were once domesticated. They were fed and cared for by their human handlers. Humans also helped to protect them from wild animals that might cause them harm. Some horses separated from these domesticated herds. They had to find new ways to survive on their own. This meant developing adaptations to help them locate food and water and avoid predators.

Most domesticated horses are fed regularly and receive routine grooming.

Finding Food and Water

Unlike domesticated animals, wild horses do not have a guaranteed food or water supply. As a result, some herds travel up to 20 miles (32 km) a day to locate land where they can graze. Grass can sometimes be hard to find. Wild horses feed on whatever plant life is available in these situations. They have been known to eat leaves, twigs, and tree bark. They also lick or eat soil to absorb extra minerals that their bodies need to stay healthy.

Wild horses drink freshwater from ponds, streams, springs, lakes, and rivers. They sometimes paw at the ground with their hooves to dig past snow, rocks, or soil that is covering a water hole. Wild horses in deserts and other dry areas have been known to chew on plants such as the prickly pear cactus. The juices inside certain fruits and berries provide them with extra moisture when their water supply is limited.

FUN FACT! Some wild horses use their hooves to uncover water up to 3 feet (0.9 m) underground.

Wild horses feed on grasses and a variety of other wild plant life.

Slow to Grow

Most domesticated horses are fully grown by the time they are three to four years old. It sometimes takes wild horses a little longer to reach their adult size. Scientists believe that this is probably another adaptation to life in the wilderness.

A wild horse's body must respond to demands that domesticated horses do not usually face. For example, American mustangs experience less physical growth when the temperature drops. These wild horses have to work harder to find food during colder months. They are also outside all the time. This means they must produce more body heat to keep warm.

A mustang uses all its energy looking for its next meal and surviving the cold weather. There is not much left over to support any major physical changes. As a result, mustangs mainly grow during spring and summer. This is why it takes longer for them to reach their full size.

Wild horses' bodies have adapted to the demands of living outside during harsh winter months.

Made to Move in the Wilderness

Wild horses are built to survive in a rugged and often unpredictable **environment**. Their smaller size allows for quick and easy movement. This is an important adaptation for animals that travel often and face wild predators.

A wild horse's bones are usually stronger and more solid than those of domesticated breeds. This allows them to run hard and fast, with less risk of injury. In addition, wild horses have extremely tough, thick hooves that help them walk and run across many different surfaces. Thinner or more delicate hooves would make it difficult for them to travel regularly along rocky or uneven ground.

A horse's hooves never stop growing, but running and walking wear them down so they do not get too long. Such activities also keeps horses' **tendons** and muscles healthy and strong. Wild horses have to be in excellent physical condition to cope with the challenges of living in a wild habitat.

Unlike their domesticated relatives, wild horses sometimes need to move quickly to avoid predators.

Sight, Sound, and Smell

Wild horses must rely on their senses to survive. A horse's eyesight is not quite as sharp as that of a human. Even so, the animal can view certain colors, slight motions, and changes in light. Scientists believe that wild horses have greater difficulty seeing objects up close than from a distance. However, the horses can spot predators from far away. This is more important than being able to see them when they are already near enough to attack.

Horses have excellent hearing. They can even detect certain sounds that people do not notice. In addition, they use their powerful sense of smell to identify and locate other members of their herd and approaching enemies. Some scientists think that wild horses may have more sensitive noses than their domesticated relatives do.

FUN FACT! Horses can swivel their ears to hear in different directions without moving their heads.

A horse's ears, eyes, and nose help it stay aware of its surroundings.

CHAPTER 3

Life in the Herd

A wild horse's social behavior is just as important to its survival as any of its physical adaptations. Even in captivity, most horses prefer to spend time in groups. For wild horses, being part of a herd increases the chances of staying alive.

Wolves, hyenas, bears, and wild cats are all possible threats. Horses that are very young, very old, sick, or injured are at the greatest risk of becoming prey. Staying with a herd is the main way these horses protect themselves from being attacked. Younger, stronger horses can help defend them from threats.

A herd of wild horses is also known as a mob or a harem. It is usually made up of a variety of smaller family groups called bands. The bands in a herd share a common home range. Herds range in size from tens to hundreds of horses. Bands are made up of anywhere from 2 to 20 horses.

Some herds of wild horses are extremely large.

Roles, Ranks, and Responsibilities

Wild horses live according to a social hierarchy. This means that each animal holds a certain position within a group. Each band is typically led by a dominant mare, or adult female horse. The rest of the band is usually made up of other mares, foals, younger horses between one and three years old, and a head stallion. Bands sometimes also feature a few males that are not as dominant as the head stallion.

The head stallion usually moves behind the rest of the group when it travels. It is his responsibility to keep a lookout for danger and guard females from other stallions within the herd. The dominant mare stays near the front of the band. It is her job to find safe areas where the band can graze and drink water.

A band of wild horses often changes members. It is not uncommon for horses to leave and join different groups within the herd. Sometimes wild horses challenge other members of the band for social dominance.

Younger horses learn to follow the lead of older herd members.

Close Bonds

The head stallion **mates** with the mares in his band. Mating occurs at different times of the year depending on what part of the world the horses live in. Females are pregnant for approximately 11 to 12 months. They give birth to either a single foal or, occasionally, a pair of twins. Babies stand, walk, and are ready to travel with the rest of the herd in a matter of hours.

Wild baby horses nurse, or drink their mother's milk, for around two years. They also begin feeding on grass when they are between two and four weeks old. A baby horse shares a close bond with its mother. Mares and foals nuzzle each other to show affection. Wild horses also communicate by making noises that include whinnies, snorts, squeals, and even screams. These sounds are used to alert the band of danger, greet other horses, and express emotions.

FUN FACT! Baby horses can run and swim within a single day of being born.

Foals tend to be extremely affectionate toward their mothers.

A Look at a Life Span

Female horses that are less than four years old are called fillies. Young males are known as colts. Fillies usually break away from their families to join separate bands when they are between two and three years old. Most colts leave at roughly the same age. They form small groups with the herd's other young males. After turning four, male horses are considered stallions. Some young stallions come together with mares to create their own bands. Others challenge older males for dominance within a band that already exists.

Wild horses start to mate between the ages of four and five. In their natural habitats, they usually live to be 10 to 15 years old. In rare cases, they can live for more than 20 years. Not every wild horse is this lucky. Predators, diseases, **parasites**, and human activity all affect a horse's ability to survive in the wilderness. Another major problem lies in the horses' teeth. As they age, their teeth slowly wear down from chewing up plants. This makes them less effective at chewing food. Horses with overly worn teeth are not able to get the amount of nutrients they need to survive.

Colts and fillies are not quite babies but are not full-grown adults either.

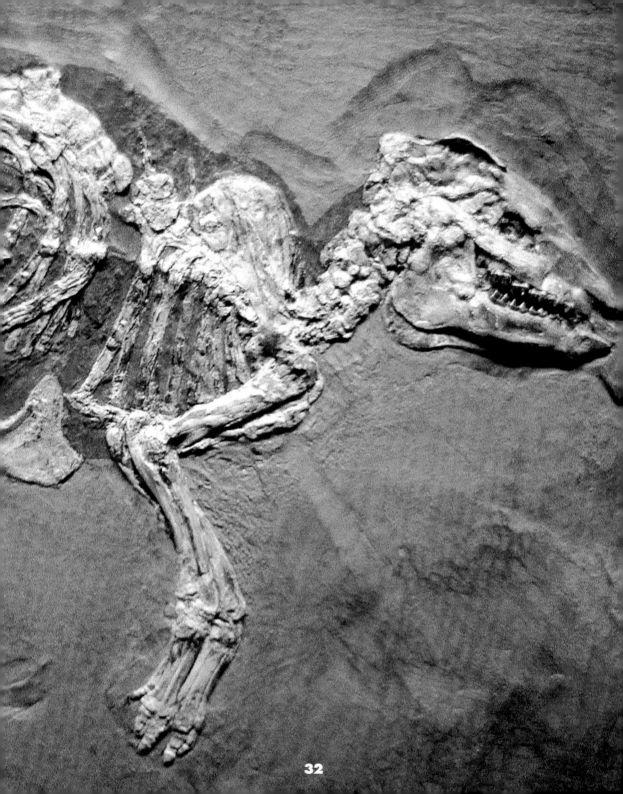

CHAPTER 4

The History of Wild Horses

Scientists think that the earliest horses appeared on Earth about 50 million years ago. **Fossils** reveal that an animal named Eohippus lived in what are now North America, Europe, and Asia. It was not much larger than a small dog but had hoofed toes and a long skull. Eohippus probably grazed on plants, much like modern horses do.

Over time, horses began to more closely resemble the animals that people are familiar with today. Humans began taming horses sometime around 4000 BCE. People were not able to domesticate all of them, though. Even those that were successfully tamed did not always stay that way. Some of them eventually ended up back in the wilderness. These once-domesticated animals mated and formed feral herds.

Fossils have helped scientists learn about ancient animals such as Eohippus.

What Led to Life in the Wild?

There are several reasons why groups of formerly domesticated horses evolved into the wild herds that roam the world today. In many cases, they either were abandoned by their owners or escaped captivity. Sometimes people purposely released tame horses into the wilderness to give them more grazing space. They planned to recapture the horses later, but they were not always successful.

Wild horses living off the eastern coasts of Maryland and Virginia can likely be traced back to an 18th-century shipwreck. Historians suspect that a boat carrying ponies from North Africa to Peru got trapped in a storm not far from Assateague Island. The animals probably swam ashore. They later mated with other breeds that were introduced to the area. These breeds included Shetland, Welsh, and Arabian ponies.

The result was the wild herds of Assateague and Chincoteague Islands. About 300 ponies still roam free there today. A much larger number have been captured and sold to private owners.

The ancestors of the wild ponies of Assateague and Chincoteague Islands may have been involved in a shipwreck several centuries ago.

Never Truly Tamed

The **species** name *Equus ferus* means "wild horses" in Latin. It is divided into three **subspecies**: domesticated horses that have gone wild, Przewalski's horses, and tarpans. Some experts consider feral horses such as mustangs and brumbies to be members of the first group. Others classify them along with domesticated horses as part of the *Equus caballus* species.

Many scientists say that the Przewalski's horse is the truest wild horse. Unlike others, it was never successfully domesticated. Some experts believe tarpans, which have been **extinct** since the early 1900s, were never truly domesticated either.

Przewalski's horses typically weigh 440 to 750 pounds (200 to 340 kg) and are about 12 to 14 hands high. They used to roam treeless plains called steppes in Mongolia and northern China. But then they completely disappeared from the wild. Only captive ones remained. Scientists have recently reintroduced the Przewalski's horse to the Mongolian wilderness. Unfortunately, only about 300 of them currently live in the wild.

Przewalski's horses have never been domesticated.

CHAPTER 5

Destined to Disappear?

Human beings share a complicated relationship with wild horses. Many herds graze on the same lands that farmers want to use for their sheep and cattle. Some people argue that the horses trample plant life and soil that other wild animals depend on to survive. Such conflicts are further complicated by the fact that wild herds are often able to grow rapidly.

A common response to these concerns is the culling of wild horses. Culling involves either killing or capturing large numbers of horses. Sometimes captured horses are eventually released in new locations in the wild. Others face death or life in captivity.

People who support culling say that it keeps herd populations at manageable sizes. That way, they do not threaten either farmland or natural habitats. Others oppose the killing or capture of wild horses. They believe that these animals have a right to roam free.

Some ranchers fear that wild horses will eat the grasses that their livestock need to survive.

Facing an Uncertain Future

Scientists say that 2 million American mustangs roamed the United States in 1900. Their numbers have dropped to about 30,000 a little more than a century later. The United States and other nations have laws in place to protect wild horses. But many farmers and government officials are still worried about the impact that wild horses have on grazing land and local wildlife. Many conservationists have tried to come up with solutions that address these concerns and protect wild herds.

For example, some people have opened sanctuaries where wild horses can run free in their natural habitat. Others support the idea of treating the animals with drugs that stop them from reproducing. Many conservationists are educating the public about the horses' past, present, and uncertain future. Wild horses are more than symbols of freedom and natural beauty. These animals are also living creatures worthy of respect and a place in the wild.

Wild horses that live on sanctuaries are protected from human threats.

Words to Know

adapted (uh-DAP-tid) — changed in order to fit a new setting or set of circumstances

ancestors (AN-ses-turz) — ancient animal species that are related to modern species

breeds (BREEDZ) — groups of animals that share common ancestors and similar traits

captivity (kap-TIV-i-tee) — the condition of being held or trapped by people

conservationists (kon-sur-VAY-shun-ists) — people who work to protect an environment and the living things in it

domesticated (duh-MES-tih-kay-tid) — tamed and kept as a pet or farm animal

dominant (DAH-muh-nint) — most influential or powerful

environment (en-VYE-ruhn-mint) — surroundings in which an animal lives or spends time

equine (EE-kwine) — related to horses

extinct (ik-STINGKT) — no longer found alive

feral (FARE-uhl) — formerly captive and currently living in the wild

foals (FOHLZ) — baby horses

fossils (FOSS-uhlz) — the hardened remains of prehistoric plants and animals

graze (GRAYZ) — feed on grasses or other plants

groom (GROOM) — to clean an animal's fur or skin

habitats (HAB-uh-tats) — the places where an animal or a plant is usually found

herd (HURD) — a group of animals that stay together or move together hierarchy (HYE-ur-ahr-kee) — a social system in which animals have different ranks or levels of importance

home range (HOME RAYNJ) — area of land in which animals spend most of their time

mates (MAYTS) — joins together to produce babies

minerals (MIN-ur-uhlz) — substances that the body needs for good health and that are not made of plant or animal matter

parasites (PAR-uh-sites) — animals or plants that live on or inside of another animal or plant

predators (PREH-duh-turz) — animals that live by hunting other animals for food

prey (PRAY) — an animal that's hunted by another animal for food

sanctuaries (SANGK-choo-er-eez) — natural areas where animals are protected from hunters or other dangers

species (SPEE-sheez) — one of the groups into which animals and plants of the same genus are divided

stallions (STAL-yunz) — adult male horses above the age of four that are capable of breeding

subspecies (SUHB-spee-sheez) — groups of animals that are part of the same species but share important differences

tendons (TEN-duhnz) — strong, thick cords or bands of tissue that join muscles to bones or other body parts

ungulates (UNG-yuh-luhts) — hoofed mammals such as horses

Habitat Map

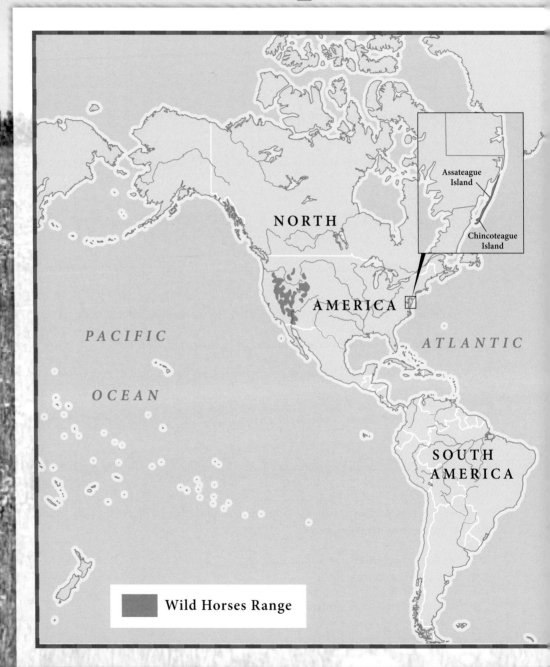

NORTH
AMERICA

Assateague
Island

Chincoteague
Island

PACIFIC

OCEAN

ATLANTIC

SOUTH
AMERICA

Wild Horses Range

ARCTIC OCEAN

EUROPE

ASIA

AFRICA

PACIFIC OCEAN

OCEAN

INDIAN

OCEAN

AUSTRALIA

Find Out More

Books

Frazel, Ellen. *The Spanish Mustang*. Minneapolis: Bellwether Media, 2012.

Frydenborg, Kathryn. *The Wild Horse Scientists*. Boston: Houghton Mifflin Harcourt, 2013.

Magby, Meryl. *Mustangs*. New York: PowerKids Press, 2012.

Visit this Scholastic Web site for more information on wild horses:
www.factsfornow.scholastic.com
Enter the keywords **Wild Horses**

Index

Page numbers in *italics* indicate a photograph or map.

About the Author

Katie Marsico is the author of more than 100 children's books. She hopes to eventually visit one of the islands along the East Coast where wild horses continue to roam free. Ms. Marsico is grateful to her dear friend Russell Primm for giving her yet another opportunity to write about a fascinating subject.